Unlocking the Secrets of Science

Profiling 20th Century Achievers in Science, Medicine, and Technology

Linus Pauling and the Chemical Bond

•••

Susan Zannos

PO Box 619 • Bear, Delaware 19701
www.mitchelllane.com

Unlocking the Secrets of Science

Profiling 20th Century Achievers in Science, Medicine, and Technology

Linus Pauling and the Chemical Bond

Mitchell Lane
PUBLISHERS

Copyright © 2004 by Mitchell Lane Publishers, Inc. All rights reserved. No part of this book may be reproduced without written permission from the publisher. Printed and bound in the United States of America.

Printing   1   2   3   4   5   6   7   8   9   10

Library of Congress Cataloging-in-Publication Data
Zannos, Susan
      Linus Pauling and the Chemical Bond/Susan Zannos.
        p. cm. — (Unlocking the secrets of science)
      Summary: Profiles the Nobel Prize-winning chemist who described the nature of chemical bonds and made other important discoveries in the fields of quantum mechanics and immunology.
      Includes bibliographical references and index.
      ISBN 1-58415-123-4 (lib)
      1. Pauling, Linus, 1901—Juvenile literature. 2. Biochemists—United States—Biography—Juvenile literature. 3. Chemists—United States—Biography—Juvenile literature. 4. Chemical bonds—Juvenile literature. [1. Pauling, Linus, 1901- 2. Chemists. 3. Nobel Prizes—Biography.] I. Title. II. Series.
QD22.P35 Z36 2002
540'.92—dc21
[B]   2002025455

ABOUT THE AUTHOR: Susan Zannos has been a lifelong educator, having taught at all levels, from preschool to college, in Mexico, Greece, Italy, Russia, and Lithuania, as well as in the United States. She has published a mystery *Trust the Liar* (Walker and Co.) and *Human Types: Essence and the Enneagram* (Samuel Weiser). Her book, *Human Types*, was recently translated into Russian, and in 2003 Susan was invited to tour Russia and lecture about her book. She has also written many books for children, including *Chester Carlson and the Development of Xerography* and *The Life and Times of Franz Joseph Haydn* (Mitchell Lane). When not traveling, Susan lives in the Sierra Foothills of Northern California.

CHILDREN'S SCIENCE REVIEW EDITOR: Stephanie Kondrchek, B.S. Microbiology, University of Maryland

PHOTO CREDITS: cover: Photo Researchers; p. 6 Hulton/Archive; p. 10 Barbara Marvis; p. 14 Photo Researchers; p. 18 Library of Congress; p. 23 Corbis; p. 24 Corbis; p. 29 Photo Researchers; p. 30 Library of Congress; pp. 32, 33, 34 Caltech; p. 35 Cold Spring Harbor Laboratory; p. 36 Getty Images

PUBLISHER'S NOTE: In selecting those persons to be profiled in this series, we first attempted to identify the most notable accomplishments of the 20th century in science, medicine, and technology. When we were done, we noted a serious deficiency in the inclusion of women. For the greater part of the 20th century, science, medicine, and technology were male-dominated fields. In many cases, the contributions of women went unrecognized. Women have tried for years to be included in these areas, and in many cases, women worked side by side with men who took credit for their ideas and discoveries. Even as we move forward into the 21st century, we find women still sadly underrepresented. It is not an oversight, therefore, that we profiled mostly male achievers. Information simply does not exist to include a fair selection of women.

      This story is based on the author's extensive research, which she believes to be accurate. Documentation of that research can be found on p. 46.

      The internet sites referenced in this book were all active as of the date of publication. Due to the fleeting nature of some Web sites, we cannot guarantee they will all be active when you are reading this book.

Contents

Dmitri Ivanovich Mendeleev was born in Tobolsk, Siberia in 1834 and educated in St. Petersburg. A brilliant scientist, he felt that there was some kind of order to the elements. He spent over 13 years gathering data that lead to his greatest accomplishment, the Periodic Table of Elements.

Chapter 1

Off With a Bang

The first laboratory that Linus Pauling had was in the basement of his mother's boarding house in Portland, Oregon. A boarding house is a place where people pay to stay. Linus and his friend Lloyd Jeffress collected every bit of equipment and chemical supplies they could lay their hands on to use in the lab.

Linus's grandfather, who lived in the small town of Oswego a few miles south of Portland, worked as night watchman for an abandoned iron smelter (a place where iron ore was refined). There was a small deserted laboratory at the smelter that still had boxes of old chemicals and some rusting equipment. Linus moved the contents of this laboratory to his basement. He took apart a machine for distilling, or purifying water, and put the pieces into suitcases to carry back on the train. He and his friend managed to get an electric heater into a canoe and paddled it down the Willamette River. From there they used a wheelbarrow to get it the rest of the way to the boarding house.

Linus and Lloyd spent long hours in their basement laboratory, which they had built out of pieces of scrap lumber. It had a door with a lock on it so that Linus's mother and sisters could not get in. One afternoon the boys mixed chemicals together that would make a loud explosion but would not actually harm anything. They put a jar full of their mixture on the trolley tracks and waited behind some bushes until the trolley came. The huge bang scared the trolley riders and everyone in the neighborhood. It delighted the two boys. Their experiment had been a great success.

Linus wanted to learn everything he could about chemistry. He wanted to know how the world fit together and how it worked. This was during the early 1900s when scientists all over the world were studying chemistry. There was still a lot to learn about the mysterious nature of substances that make up everything in the world.

Chemists knew that *atoms* were the smallest units of matter. They knew that certain substances, called *elements*, were made up of atoms that were all alike and were different from the atoms of all other elements. By the middle of the 1800s, chemists had begun to find patterns in the way elements behaved. In 1869 a Russian chemist named Mendeleev published his *periodic table* that arranged the elements in order of atomic weight. He left gaps for the elements that hadn't been discovered yet but that he was sure would be. He was right. More elements would later be discovered.

Chemists also knew that atoms combined to form *molecules*. A molecule is the smallest particle of a substance that can exist by itself and still have all the characteristics of that substance. The molecules of elements are formed from atoms that are all alike. On the other hand, *compounds* were made up of atoms that had combined to produce substances that were very different from any of the elements they were made of. Water, for example, is made up of hydrogen and oxygen. But it is not like hydrogen or oxygen, which are both usually gases. When two hydrogen atoms and one oxygen atom join together, they form water. Whatever happens to water it continues to be water. It can be frozen into ice, a solid. It can be boiled into steam, a gas. But it is still water. It doesn't retain the properties of hydrogen or oxygen.

Ordinary table salt is another compound. Salt is made of sodium, which is a silvery metallic element, and chlorine, a smelly green gas. The resulting compound can be heated, dissolved in water and then frozen, placed under pressure, mixed up with other substances, and it is still salt. It doesn't come apart into the elements of sodium and chlorine.

In other substances, the elements may mix together, but they can be easily separated. These substances are called *mixtures*. Water and salt are both compounds. When water and salt are mixed together, the salt dissolves completely so it is not visible, but it can still be tasted. It is evenly distributed throughout the volume of water. It is easy to separate these two compounds. When the mixture of salt and water is boiled, the water becomes a gas. The salt is left behind in its original form as a solid. The two compounds have been separated.

The experiments that Linus and Lloyd performed in the boarding house basement made great explosions and horrible smells. This was a lot of fun. But for Linus it was more than fun. He wanted to know why things happened the way they did. Why was it that when he put some things together they stayed together, but when he put other things together they came apart again? And why could some things be combined but others couldn't?

Linus wanted to learn. He wanted to learn everything he possibly could learn. He faced many large obstacles but he never really considered any other possibility than continuing his experiments throughout his life.

The natural beauty of Oregon state where Linus Pauling grew up created a sense of wonder in the boy. He wanted to learn everything he could about the substances that make up the world. He collected insects and minerals and classified them, but his main interest was chemistry; he wanted to know how the world worked.

Chapter 2

Determined to Learn

Linus Pauling was born on February 28, 1901, in Portland, Oregon. His father, Herman Pauling, was a druggist who didn't earn enough to support his family after his son and two daughters were born. Herman moved his wife Belle, and children, Linus, Pauline, and Lucille, to the little town of Oswego where his parents lived. But again he could not earn a living.

The Pauling family moved again, this time to be near Linus's mother's parents in eastern Oregon. In the little town of Condon, Herman Pauling started a drugstore.

By this time Linus was five years old. He began school in the one-room schoolhouse in Condon. Linus's cousin, Mervyn Stephenson, lived on a wheat ranch near Condon where Linus frequently visited. The boys wandered the fields, explored the hedgerows and skipped stones in the streams. In the winter when it was bitterly cold, they would take refuge in the back room of the drugstore and watch Linus's father mix medicines for his customers.

When Linus was nine years old, the family moved again, this time back to Portland where Herman again opened a drugstore. Linus missed his cousin Mervyn, but by then he had discovered books. He read every book in his house and then borrowed books from neighbors. His father recognized that his son had an extraordinary mind, but didn't have the background to suggest a course of reading for him.

In June 1910, Herman died suddenly. The loss of his father was a great shock to young Linus. Although Herman left no money, the legacy he left his son was of more value. He had encouraged Linus and had respected his studies.

Linus's mother did not share her husband's attitude toward education. She saw no use for it. Belle Pauling ran a boarding house to support her three children, and she put constant pressure on Linus to help her earn money. Linus did help his mother. He set pins in a bowling alley after school to earn money and did chores around the boarding house. Linus did not help as much as his mother thought he should, however. He didn't stop reading and collecting insects and minerals. He built his own workspace in the basement of the house where he could be alone to read, classify his collections, think and study without interruptions, and conduct experiments. He also sometimes visited an elderly man, Mr. Yocum, who lived around the corner. Mr. Yocum told Linus that he needed to study Greek, and began teaching him.

By the time Linus entered high school in 1913, he knew some Greek, was able to speak German, which he had learned from his father's parents, and had poured over the two books his father had used in his work, *Pharmacopoeia of the United States* and *The Dispensatory of the United States*. These books gave detailed descriptions of the drugs used in the early 1900s and suggested medicines for hundreds of diseases. They were the foundation of Linus's fascination with science.

Linus enjoyed visiting his friend Lloyd Jeffress's family because they were educated people who talked about books and ideas at the dinner table. The Jeffress's house was very different from the Pauling boarding house with its rough working class boarders who talked only of sports and their jobs.

The more time Linus devoted to his studies and experiments, the more intense the conflicts with his mother became. He worked hard to earn money. He got up early to deliver milk, worked after school and at night operating motion picture projectors, and for a while worked in the local shipyards. But he made no secret of his intention to go to college, which his mother opposed.

The Jeffress family supported Linus's decision, pointing out that he would eventually be able to earn much more when he was a college graduate than he could possibly earn with only a high school education. In 1917, when he was sixteen years old, Linus was accepted to Oregon Agricultural College. The college accepted him early in his senior year of high school on the basis of his good grades and his background in science. As it turned out, Linus never actually finished high school because he was missing a required social studies credit. Linus is probably the only high school dropout who ever won a Nobel Prize, much less two of them.

Before leaving for college Linus wrote in his diary, "I will not be able, on account of my youth and inexperience, to do justice to the courses and the teaching placed before me." That may well have been the last instance in which he ever had any doubts about his own abilities.

Linus Pauling began his successful teaching career while he was still an undergraduate at Oregon Agricultural College. He liked teaching and he was good at it.

Chapter 3

College

When Linus Pauling arrived at Oregon Agricultural College on a Saturday afternoon in October 1917, one of the first people he saw was his cousin Mervyn. The two friends roomed together in a boarding house near the campus. The money Linus had saved from his jobs saw him through the first five months of college. Then he worked in a girls' dorm chopping wood and mopping floors. Although he was working hard, he didn't mind. He was used to working hard. Being away from his mother's nagging about money made life a lot easier.

Even though Linus was younger than most other college students, he soon discovered that he knew as much, or more, about chemistry than many of his professors. He got all As in his science and math courses. Any doubts he may have had about his abilities were gone forever. During his second year of college, Linus got a job that was more to his liking. He worked for the chemistry department preparing chemicals for use in the labs.

Also in his sophomore year, he began to enjoy more of a social life. He joined a student group called a fraternity. His fraternity brothers had a rule that anyone who didn't have a date on Saturday night had to get dunked in a bathtub full of cold water. Linus hadn't found a girl that he liked enough to ask out, so he got dunked. When he'd had enough of that, he came up with a plan. He took several fast deep breaths, and then when the other college boys dunked him, he lay very still under the water holding his breath. It gave them quite a scare. After that Linus was never dunked again.

After his sophomore year, Linus got the best job he'd had so far. He worked for the State of Oregon testing the asphalt used in building the highway system. He liked being out with the road crews, learning surveying and how to operate machinery. He sent the money he earned to his mother, asking her to use some for her needs and put the rest aside for his college expenses. But when the summer was over, Belle Pauling told her son that she had spent all of the money and needed more. She said he would have to continue working.

If his mother's intention was to get Linus to quit college, she failed. He did get another job, however. His chemistry professors got him a job teaching the introductory chemistry class. For an undergraduate student to teach a college course was highly unusual, but then, so was Linus Pauling. Linus had always been critical of his own professors. He had little patience with teachers who were boring or were not well prepared for their classes. He felt that he had to prove to his own students that having someone their own age as an instructor did not shortchange them. Linus was well prepared to teach. Not only did he know a lot about chemistry, he had also studied public speaking. Linus was actually a better teacher than many of the professors. Word spread and students were enrolling early to get into his classes. Linus liked teaching and was good at it.

Linus's year of full time teaching was important in other ways. He had a desk assigned to him in the chemistry library, and he got access to the newest chemistry journals. By reading them Linus learned about the latest research. By the time he returned to his studies in his junior year he had gained so much self-confidence that some of his classmates thought he was arrogant.

For all his academic and teaching success, Linus still was rather shy around girls and didn't date. He was nervous when he found that he had been assigned to teach a chemistry course to home economics majors. It was the winter term of 1922, and he would have twenty-five young ladies in the class. On the first day of class, Linus started by finding out what his students already knew about chemistry. He called on Ava Helen Miller to answer the first question. Her name was one that he knew he could pronounce. As it turned out, she knew a lot about the subject of his question, but it is not certain that her young teacher even heard her answer. If there was ever a case of love at first sight, Linus had just experienced it.

Linus pretended to ignore this pretty, dark-haired, and very bright girl. He knew that it was against college policy for instructors to become romantically involved with their students. Ava Helen, however, knew exactly what was going on and flirted with her handsome young teacher. Linus bent over backwards to give Ava Helen grades lower than she deserved to be sure that he wasn't showing favoritism. This made Ava Helen furious. Finally Linus just gave up and asked her to go for a walk with him. It was the first of many long walks together. By late spring he asked her to marry him. She said yes.

The German-born mathematician and physicist Albert Einstein visited and lectured at Caltech while Linus Pauling was a graduate student there. On one occasion, Pauling presented a paper while Einstein was visiting, and to show his respect he delivered the paper in flawless German.

Chapter 4
Graduate School

Ava Helen Miller opened Linus Pauling's mind as well as his heart. During their long talks, she shared her interest in the social and political issues that had always been discussed in her family. At his graduation ceremony in the spring of 1922, Linus gave the senior oration in which he voiced his belief that the educated man had a duty to serve humanity by attempting to solve social problems. The new direction his interests were taking as a result of his relationship with Ava Helen made him determined to go to graduate school and become a university professor. He felt he could best serve by solving the problems that were baffling chemists.

The decision to go to graduate school was not an easy one. His mother begged him to return home and get a job teaching and help support his family. More difficult was the prospect of being separated from Ava Helen. Her mother as well as his opposed their marrying then. Ava Helen's family wanted her to complete her college degree.

Linus's decision about what graduate school to go to was not easy either. He knew that his success depended on being able to work with the top researchers in the field, and he knew where they were—mostly at big established universities like Harvard and Berkeley.Linus was particularly interested in the ideas of Dr. Gilbert Lewis, the head of the chemistry department at Berkeley.

Dr. Lewis thought that the bonding of atoms to form molecules occurred because the structures of atoms were incomplete. He thought atoms were stable when their outer shell that surrounded the *nucleus,* or center of the atom, contained eight *electrons.* If there were fewer than eight, Lewis theorized, the atom would attempt to join with another atom that had extra electrons. The shared electrons would then bind the atoms together into molecules. Linus thought that Dr. Lewis was on the right track.

Nonetheless, Linus took a gamble and chose the California Institute of Technology, known as Caltech. It was a new chemistry department in a young school with a small campus in Pasadena. But it had as department chairman Arthur Noyes, an internationally known chemical theorist and an excellent teacher. Noyes had come to Caltech because he had been guaranteed a new laboratory and the ability to develop the chemistry department as he wished.

Noyes created a program that brought students and professors together in seminars and in activities such as camping trips. He would make Caltech an internationally famous center for the study of chemistry. Linus would be the most important of the many scholars in the chemistry department at Caltech.

One feature of the program was that all the chemists—professors and students—had Tuesday and Thursday meetings in which the senior professors would decide on a topic to present. They would go much more deeply into it than they could in a classroom. Sometimes great scientists from other institutions would be invited to participate.

It was at one of these meetings that Linus met Albert Einstein. One of the other participants told Tom Hager (*Linus Pauling and the Chemistry of Life*), "Einstein came over here and attended a scientific meeting and at the end of the meeting Linus was to deliver a paper. He delivered a paper in flawless German." Einstein was very impressed. The incident was typical of the care Linus always took to prepare himself for important occasions.

The two most important things that happened during Linus's graduate studies at Caltech were starting a family and learning a procedure called *X-ray crystallography*. Ava Helen made it clear that she wasn't going to wait around in Oregon while Linus was having an exciting life in California. Linus agreed that the two would get married the summer after his first year at Caltech. He had his summer job testing asphalt again, and the young couple traveled with the road crew up and down the back roads of Oregon. In the fall they found a small house near Caltech. They had very little money, but Ava Helen was a good manager with what little they had. She was far too bright and restless to sit home alone, so she frequently attended classes with Linus and spent a lot of time in the laboratory helping with measurements, diagrams, calculations, and laboratory notes.

Each graduate student was assigned to work with one of the major professors. Linus worked with Dr. Roscoe Dickinson who was an expert in the new technique of X-ray crystallography. The atoms of solids form repeating patterns. When an X-ray beam is directed at the crystals of a solid, the ray is broken up, forming a pattern. From analyzing the pattern, the researcher could work out the distances and angles between the atoms that the crystals were made of. Before this technique was developed, scientists only guessed at the way that atoms joined together to form molecules. With X-ray crystallography the structures of simple crystals could be verified.

Professor Dickinson helped Linus prepare thin slices of the compound molybdenite and showed him how to operate the delicate X-ray equipment. Working together, Linus and Dickinson were able to determine the atomic structure of molybdenite. It was Linus' first laboratory success, and he was thrilled. Later he wrote, "I was pleased to learn that questions about the nature of the world could be answered by carefully planned and executed experiments." He went on to discover the atomic structures of four more crystals, which was an amazing feat for a graduate student.

1925 was an important year for Linus. He earned his doctorate degree with honors from Caltech, and in March his son, Linus, Jr. was born. Just after the baby was born, the Paulings learned that Linus had been awarded a Guggenheim Fellowship to study *physics* in Europe. Physics is a science that studies matter and motion. Early in 1926 Linus and Ava Helen left the baby with her mother and went to Germany where Linus studied under one of the world's leading physicists, Arnold Sommerfield.

At that time the University of Munich was at the center of exciting new theories about atomic structure. Seemingly conflicting theories were being proposed to explain the way subatomic particles behaved. One theory was that particles orbited the nucleus of an atom like planets orbited the sun. Another theory said the particles were like waves surrounding the nucleus. But whichever way the particles were described as moving, the mathematical equations used by physicists to describe them explained the way atoms actually functioned. The theories were combined under the name *quantum mechanics*.

The new physics provided Linus with the second of the major tools he would use to discover the structures of molecules. The first was X-ray crystallography and the second was quantum mechanics. Throughout his incredibly productive career, Linus would formulate his theories through his intuitive understanding of how atoms bonded with other atoms. He would then use X-ray crystallography to see if the patterns formed in the X-rays proved his theory. And finally he calculated equations of quantum mechanics to be sure the particles were behaving the way his theory predicted that they would.

Linus Pauling's Guggenheim Fellowship to study in Germany in 1926 enabled him to study the new field of quantum mechanics. When he returned to Caltech, students flocked to his classes for his clear explanations of this theory and its complex calculations.

In 1954 Linus Pauling was awarded the Nobel Prize for Chemistry. The award came at a time in his career when he was under attack for his efforts to prevent nuclear testing. He shares his delight with his family: (left to right) his daughter-in-law Anita, his daughter Linda, and his wife Ava Helen.

Chapter 5

Early Career

When Linus and Ava Helen returned from Europe in the fall of 1927, Caltech was growing. There were new departments of geology and biology, and important visitors like Albert Einstein kept everyone up-to-date on scientific ideas. It was an exciting place for a new assistant professor of chemistry. Linus was 26 years old. He had his first office and he was a popular teacher both for his informal but clear teaching methods and his knowledge of the new ideas in quantum physics.

Linus' first interest, however, was not in teaching but in research. He set out to discover the structures of a family of minerals called silicates. He knew that the silicates—which included topaz, talc, and mica—were composed of silicon, oxygen, and a few metal atoms. He knew that silicon had a valence of four. This meant that it typically bonded to four other atoms, forming a four-sided pyramid called a tetrahedron. Oxygen, on the other hand, frequently formed an octahedron, a cube shape.

Linus and Ava Helen drew pictures on paper. Then they cut and folded paper into the three-dimensional shapes and sewed them together. It was like a game that had very strict rules. The sizes of the atoms had to match what was known about them. The positions of the bonds had to match what had been discovered by X-ray crystallography. And the positive and negative electrical charges of neighboring ions had to balance out. The mathematical equations had to conform to the newly discovered laws of quantum mechanics.

Linus's imagination was controlled by the chemical rules he knew. The models he created fitted logically and seemed the only possible way the molecules could be constructed. Using these paper models, Linus discovered the structures of mica, talc, and topaz and other minerals that had been considered too complex to understand.

In 1928 Linus published the guidelines he had used to solve the mystery of the silicates. Pauling's Rules, as they were called, showed researchers all over the world a new way to study complex crystal structures. It was an important success and created an international reputation for Linus. He was offered an important faculty position at Harvard, but turned it down because he wanted to stay in California.

Linus wanted to apply the same method that he had used for the silicates to larger molecules. Other scientists in Europe and America were working on the same problem, and he remained aware of their progress. Most of the others were physicists who could describe the patterns that the electrons made. In the carbon molecule, for example, the orbits of some of the electrons were not circular but oval. Linus scribbled and drew pictures, he worked mathematical equations and came up with theories, but for two years nothing worked.

As a chemist, Linus knew that carbon usually formed four equal bonds to create a tetrahedron. As a physicist, he knew that no four electrons in a carbon atom were the same. How could both those things be true? Finally, the equations started to work. He had used the principles of the quantum mechanics he had learned in Germany to describe the binding of carbon. He didn't stop there. He added more

Date Due Receipt

Author: Silverstein, Alvin.
Title: Frederick Sanger;
the man who mapped out
a chemic
Item ID:
39082034462212
Date due: 8/24/2010,23:
59

Author: Zannos, Susan.
Title: Linus Pauling and
the chemical bond
Item ID:
39082101633975
Date due: 8/24/2010,23:
59

Fines may be charged if
items
are not returned by due
date.
Renew items at:
catalog.lhl.lib.mt.us

electrons to his calculations and found the structures of more complicated molecules.

In the biography by Tom Hager, Linus is quoted as saying, "I was so excited and happy, I think I stayed up all night, making, writing out, solving the equations, which were so simple I could solve them in a few minutes. Solve one equation, get the answer, then solve another equation. . . . I just kept getting more and more euphorius as time went by." Linus sent the results to the *Journal of the American Chemical Society* in a paper titled "The Nature of the Chemical Bond." Again Linus's work gained attention from around the world. The American Chemical Society awarded him the Langmuir Prize as the best young chemist in America. At Caltech he was promoted to full professor at age 30.

Linus's great success was the result of hard work. Linus combined his theories with laboratory experiments. He didn't rely on his ideas alone—although he certainly had a lot of ideas. And he didn't rely on making lots and lots of experiments and adding up the results. He did both, but the ideas came first and the proof by experiments and calculations came afterwards.

As Linus's success and fame grew, so did his self-confidence. In fact, some of the other faculty members at Caltech thought Pauling's self-confidence had grown entirely too much. He had a big new office, more assistants than anyone else, and spent a lot of time traveling all over the country lecturing at other universities. Linus's family was also growing. A son, Peter, was born in 1931 and a daughter, Linda, in 1932.

Arthur Noyes, the man who had created the world famous Caltech chemistry department, died in 1936. Before he died, he made clear that he thought Linus was the man to succeed him. But after the Noyes died, many of the older members of the department said they didn't want Linus as department head. For months the position went unfilled, which confused and angered Linus.

It took a powerful outsider, the head of the natural sciences division of the world's wealthiest foundation, the Rockefeller Foundation, to overcome the opposition to Linus Pauling at Caltech. This man, Warren Weaver, was particularly interested in applying the techniques of chemistry and physics to biology. He felt that Linus was exactly the scientist who would be able to do this. Weaver called the field he wanted to spend money on "molecular biology." He made it clear that if Linus were the head of the chemistry department at Caltech, the Rockefeller money would be available for funding. In 1937 Linus was named department chairman. In the same year his fourth and last child, Edward Crellin, was born.

In spite of the complaints of the older members of the department, Linus did a good job. He attracted lots of money, and he continued to have success in his own research. What was even better, he wasn't at all the dictator that his colleagues had feared he would be.

In 1939 Linus published one of the most important scientific books of the twentieth century, *The Nature of the Chemical Bond and the Structure of Molecules and Crystals: An Introduction to Modern Structural Chemistry*. If he had done no more than the research and discoveries that culminated in this book, his position as a great scientist would have been guaranteed. But he did a great deal more.

Professor Pauling demonstrated the structures of molecules by constructing models that looked like tinker toys. With these he was able to show his chemistry students how chemical bonds were formed.

The huge mushroom-shaped clouds that formed from the explosion of nuclear weapons released radioactive particles into the earth's atmosphere. Linus Pauling and other scientists all over the world believed that testing of these bombs should be stopped. Pauling and his wife gave lectures and demonstrated against the bombs.

Chapter 6

The War and After

Even before the United States entered the Second World War in 1941, Linus Pauling was aware of the desperate situation in Europe. Jewish colleagues wrote seeking help in escaping the persecutions of Hitler's government. Realizing that Germany had to be stopped, Linus began speaking publicly about the issue, urging America to join other countries in the fight against the German dictator.

As the country came closer to war, the U.S. government asked scientists to help solve problems for the military. Linus went to Washington, D.C. in October of 1940 to meet with officers from the army and navy. He learned that the navy badly needed a device that would measure the oxygen level in submarines. Linus invented such a device. He knew that oxygen was the only common gas that was attracted to a magnet, and with this knowledge constructed what became known as the Pauling Oxygen Analyzer. It was soon in production at Caltech.

Under Linus's direction, the chemists at Caltech did research on explosives. The organic chemistry lab developed artificial blood plasma for the wounded. Linus traveled often to assist factories manufacturing weapons and to advise government agencies. At home Ava Helen helped in the Caltech laboratory and served as an air-raid warden. Linus, Jr. enlisted in the Air Force.

During World War II, Japanese Americans were put in camps until the war was over. The U.S. government thought they might be a threat to Americans since America was fighting against Japan in the war. The Paulings took a strong stand against the injustice of placing Japanese Americans in internment camps. The Paulings continued to employ a Japanese gardener. They were called "anti-American." For the Paulings it was the beginning of their increasing participation in unpopular political causes.

When World War II ended after the dropping of atomic bombs on Hiroshima and Nagasaki, the Paulings celebrated with the rest of America. Very soon, however, it became clear that the destruction caused by the bombs had not ended with the war. For weeks and months people in Japan continued to become ill from the radioactive particles that had been released into the air.

Furthermore, an even more powerful type of bomb, the hydrogen bomb, was being tested by the United States and by the Soviet Union. Linus and many other scientists all over the world believed that the radioactive *fallout* from

Linus Pauling took time from his experiments in chemistry to study books and articles about the world political situation. He joined other scientists who warned the public about the dangers of nuclear war.

testing the hydrogen bombs would cause many problems. They believed children would be born deformed or with brain damage. These scientists thought that the radioactive particles would contaminate the earth for thousands and thousands of years.

Linus and Ava Helen gave frequent lectures warning the American public about the dangers of testing nuclear weapons. They described the effects of nuclear fallout. They demonstrated against the bomb and proposed a world organization to ensure peace. Many people at the California Institute of Technology disagreed with the Paulings. There were some who wanted Linus fired from his position. But his brilliant scientific work continued to bring funding to the institution from the United States Public Health Service, the Rockefeller Foundation, and other groups. In 1947 Linus was elected president of the American Chemical Society. Linus's willingness to speak out strongly for what he believed made him a person with devoted friends and with bitter enemies.

Pauling lectured and demonstrated at war rallies to tell the American public about the effects of nuclear fallout. Many people at Caltech disagreed with Pauling and wanted him fired for speaking out against government policy.

While the storms of political controversy raged around him, Linus and his assistants in their laboratory at Caltech worked on discovering the complex structures of *proteins*, the building blocks of all plants and animals. They hoped that by discovering how proteins were structured they would be able to combat the diseases that occurred when proteins were defective. There are hundreds of different types of protein molecules that make up the tissues and organs in the human body. Linus and his associate Dr. Robert Corey had been working on the problem of protein structure for years without making much progress.

Then, while Linus was a guest professor at Oxford University in England in 1948, he caught a bad cold and was confined to bed for a few days. Bored, he resorted to his old game of sketching atoms and folding paper. He kept folding and twisting until he had formed a *helix*, a spiral shape that allowed bonds to be formed between one curve and the next. This was the breakthrough he had been looking for. When he returned to Caltech, he and Dr. Corey began experiments confirming that the helix was the basic shape

Robert Corey, Pauling's close associate, carried out many of the key experiments that confirmed Pauling's theories. Corey's concept of scientific progress was careful experimentation with much attention to details. Pauling said of Corey that he was "a man with a deep interest in the physical and biological world, a man who found happiness in scientific research."

of many proteins. By 1951, Linus, Corey, and physicist Herman Branson who had checked the equations, published several papers detailing the structures of proteins. The discovery of the alpha helix, as it was called, was an amazing achievement. Linus had once again led the scientific world to understandings that would change that world forever.

In May of 1952, Linus was invited to attend a conference of the Royal Society of London on the structure of proteins and the discovery of the alpha helix. He accepted with pleasure, but his pleasure turned to amazement and then anger when the State Department of the United States refused to let him go to England, saying that it was "not in the best interests of the United States." The government was reacting against his outspoken opposition to nuclear testing.

If Linus had been able to travel to England in 1952, the next year of his life probably would have been different. In England, he would have been able to talk with other physicists and chemists who were working on a complex molecule with the long name deoxyribonucleic acid, or *DNA* for short. Linus would have seen the excellent photos of the DNA molecule made by English X-ray crystallographer Rosalind Franklin.

Rosalind Franklin was a pioneer molecular biologist who was responsible for much of the research that led to the understanding of DNA.

The Nobel Prize Ceremony in the Stockholm Concert Hall in Sweden awards prizes in Physics, Chemistry, Physiology or Medicine, Literature, and Peace. The Nobel Prizes, which were first awarded in 1901, are closely linked to the development of science throughout the 20th century.

Chapter 7
Controversy and a Last Crusade

A student once asked Linus Pauling how he got so many good ideas. Linus's answer was that he had a lot of ideas and threw away the bad ones. This was usually true, but in the fall of 1952 he had a bad idea that he should have thrown away but didn't.

It had to do with DNA.

Linus, like most other biochemists at the beginning of the 1950s, believed that genetic information must be contained in some kind of protein. In the summer of 1952, Linus and other scientists learned of experiments that proved that *genes* were made of DNA. A gene is the part of DNA that contains chemical information needed to make a particular protein that controls our inherited characteristics. He immediately became interested in discovering the structure of DNA. He thought it would be simple compared to the difficulties he had encountered with the more complex protein molecules.

Never having seen the only clear X-ray crystallography photos of DNA (the ones Rosalind Franklin had taken in England), Linus began his process of sketching and manipulating models of what he thought the molecules must be like. He felt confident that he was close to another great triumph. However, his colleague Dr. Corey reported that the equations didn't work out. Nonetheless, Linus felt all that was needed were minor adjustments. Although he had only been working on the DNA structure for a month, he decided to publish his theory. That was a bad idea. He was wrong.

Two months later two researchers, James Watson and Francis Crick, at the Cavendish Laboratories of Cambridge University in England revealed their discovery of DNA structure, the now famous double helix. As soon as Linus read Watson and Crick's description of their model, he realized that they were right and sent them his congratulations. Watson and Crick won the Nobel Prize for their discovery. Mapping human genetic structure would occupy biochemists for many years to come. Linus would not be involved in it.

After the embarrassment of his hasty publication about the structure of DNA, political issues occupied much of Linus's time and energy. In spite of the harsh opposition to his views on nuclear testing, Linus continued to speak out publicly. The political climate in the United States during the 1950s was oppressive. Many people believed that the Soviet Union had organized a powerful communist conspiracy within the United States and that communists must be exposed and punished. Anyone who disagreed with government policies was thought to be a communist and an enemy of the United States. Many public figures were accused and their lives and careers ruined because they had no way of proving their innocence.

Linus was accused of being a communist "under discipline," which meant people thought he was doing what the Soviet Union told him to. This charge was ridiculous, but many people believed it. Linus always acted from his own understanding and his own beliefs.

On the first day of March in 1954, the United States blew up an entire Pacific island with a new kind of bomb a thousand times more destructive than the bombs that had destroyed Hiroshima and Nagasaki. The bomb tore a hole in the atmosphere and sent radioactive materials circling the earth. As this material started drifting back down to the surface of the planet, scientists began studying it. This fallout contained radioactive substances that had never been seen on earth before. Scientists were frightened. Linus was outraged. He continued to hold meetings and give speeches.

As Linus's anti-nuclear activities increased, so did the persecution from the U.S. government, which continued to refuse to give him permission to travel. In November 1954, Linus learned that he had been awarded the Nobel Prize in chemistry. The news was a much-needed bright spot in what had been an increasingly grim period for him. He had won an honor that was given for his entire career of accomplishment.

The Paulings applied for passports that would allow them to travel to Sweden to accept the Nobel Prize and waited anxiously for them to arrive. Finally, after pressure from the scientific community, the passports arrived. After the elegant ceremony in Stockholm, Linus gave a speech to Swedish university students that gave them advice about how to regard figures of authority: "When an old and distinguished person speaks to you, listen to him carefully and with respect—*but do not believe him.* Never put your trust in anything but your own intellect. Your elder, no matter whether he has gray hair or has lost his hair, no matter whether he is a Nobel laureate, may be wrong. . . . So you must always be skeptical—*always think for yourself.*" It was more than advice. It was a statement of Linus's philosophy.

Linus used the prestige of the Nobel Prize to reach more and more people to warn them about nuclear testing. In 1957 he sent petitions to thousands of American scientists asking them for support. He received over 2,000 signatures in two weeks, including those of other Nobel Prize winners and of members of the National Academy of Sciences. He expanded his petition drive to the scientists of the world and in a few months had gathered 9,000 more signatures. Linus and Ava Helen had accomplished this enormous task from their kitchen table. In January of 1958 he presented the entire list to the secretary-general of the United Nations. It made a big impression. People began to realize that if all of the world's scientists agreed on the danger of nuclear weapons, then the governments that claimed the testing was harmless might be wrong.

The efforts of Linus and others began to change public opinion, but they also resulted in greater pressure from the government. In 1960 a senate investigating committee told Linus he could have to go to court to testify about how he had gotten so many signatures for his petitions. He refused to cooperate, risking a prison sentence. The senate committee was harshly criticized in the world press and received hundreds of letters supporting Linus.

In 1961 President John F. Kennedy invited Linus and Ava Helen to a dinner at the White House honoring Nobel Prize winners. The same day, the Paulings demonstrated in front of the White House along with other anti-bomb protesters. They crossed their own picket lines to attend the dinner. The president told him, "I hope you will continue to express your opinions."

Finally, in 1963, the three major nuclear powers, the United States, Great Britain, and the Soviet Union, signed a treaty ending atmospheric testing of nuclear weapons. On the day the treaty went into effect, October 10, the Paulings were at their ranch in Big Sur, California, when they received the news that Linus had been awarded the Nobel Peace Prize. He became the first person ever to win two unshared Nobel Prizes.

In spite of the great honor of the Nobel Peace Prize, Linus Pauling continued to be attacked. The American press criticized the decision to give the prize to Linus. *Life* magazine called the Peace Prize "a weird insult" to America. The president of Caltech observed that many people objected to Linus's methods and activities.

In the face of negative response to the Peace Prize, Linus announced that he was leaving Caltech. When they returned from accepting the Nobel Prize, the Paulings moved to Santa Barbara where Linus joined an institution studying political and social issues. The lack of scientific facilities soon caused him to become restless and to begin searching for another field of interest. He found it in the study of the effect of vitamin therapy on brain function.

As a result of reading everything he could find about the effects of vitamins, Linus became convinced of the value of vitamin C on human health. Linus and Ava Helen began taking large doses of vitamin C every day and found that their energy increased. At Stanford University, where Linus became a consulting professor of chemistry, he conducted research into what he called the orthomolecular basis of health. The term meant having the correct balance of vitamins and other chemicals in the body.

When Linus's theory about the positive effect of large doses of vitamin C became public, he was once again the center of controversy. Doctors attacked his opinions, saying that they were without any support from scientific studies. That was not true, since there had been studies that indicated the value of vitamin C. Linus began writing of his findings, but the paper was rejected by *Science* magazine. His book *Vitamin C and the Common Cold* was published in 1970. It became a bestseller and Linus told about his work on television, radio, as well as in newspapers and magazines. Sales of vitamin C increased dramatically and manufacturers had to increase production to keep up with the public demand.

Once again the U.S. government, this time the U.S. Food and Drug Administration, opposed Linus. They issued statements saying that there was no evidence of the therapeutic value of vitamin C. The *Journal of the American Medical Association* attacked Linus for taking his theories to the public. Linus reacted to criticism as he always had, by speaking out even more strongly.

Stanford University was not pleased at having one of its professors attacked as a quack. They were also not pleased with Linus's outspoken opposition to the Vietnam War. In the early 1970s they turned down Linus's request for more space for vitamin C studies. In 1973, Linus and his assistant Art Robinson decided to open their own Institute of Orthomolecular Medicine. Supporters responded by donating hundreds of thousands of dollars to the institute, but the attacks of the medical community continued.

In 1978 Ava Helen was diagnosed with cancer. For a while massive doses of vitamin C seemed to help, but in 1981 she died. Linus was devastated by the loss of the woman who had been his partner in everything he had undertaken for nearly 60 years. Gradually, however, he began to work again. In 1986 he published his book *How to Live Longer and Feel Better.* He continued to travel and lecture, to receive awards and honorary degrees.

The evidence substantiating the value of vitamin C and other *antioxidant* vitamins—vitamins that help prevent cell damage—was accumulating. Opinion in the medical community began to change. According to Linus' biographer Tom Hager, there was a special meeting of the New York Academy of Sciences in 1992 in which studies demonstrating the usefulness of vitamin C were discussed. Near the end of the conference a professor addressed the gathering of experts: "For three days I have been listening to talks about the value of large intakes of vitamin C and other natural substances, and I have not heard a single mention of the name Linus Pauling. Has not the time come when we should admit that Linus Pauling was right all along?"

The time had indeed come. For all the controversy that surrounded him throughout his life, Linus was very seldom wrong. His theories about the nature of chemical bonding in both living and non-living molecules became the basis for modern chemistry. The world has seen the dangers of radioactive fallout that Linus warned about. The value of vitamins, particularly vitamin C, in safeguarding health are now unquestioned.

Linus Pauling died at his home in Big Sur on August 19, 1994.

Linus Pauling Chronology

1901 Linus is born February 28 in Portland, Oregon

1917 enters Oregon Agricultural College's chemical engineering program

1919 becomes a chemistry instructor at Oregon Agricultural College

1922 begins graduate studies at California Institute of Technology

1923 marries Ava Helen Miller on June 17

1925 receives doctorate from Caltech; son Linus, Jr. is born

1926 is awarded Guggenheim Fellowship to study quantum physics in Germany

1927 becomes assistant professor of chemistry at Caltech

1931 becomes full professor at Caltech; is awarded the A.C. Langmuir Prize as best young chemist in the United States; son Peter is born

1932 daughter Linda is born

1933 becomes youngest person elected to National Academy of Sciences

1937 is named chairman of Chemistry Department at Caltech; son Edward Crellin is born

1939 publishes *The Nature of the Chemical Bond* and *The Structure of Molecules and* Crystals

1946 joins the Emergency Committee of Atomic Scientists and begins anti-bomb activism

1947 publishes *General Chemistry* college textbook

1948 is invited to England as Eastman Professor at Oxford University

1949 serves as president of the American Chemical Society

1952 is labeled a communist and denied passport to travel outside of the United States

1954 is awarded Nobel Prize in Chemistry for his work on the chemical bond

1958 publishes *No More War!*; presents a petition to end nuclear testing, signed by more than 11,000 scientists, to the secretary-general of the United Nations

1963 is awarded the Nobel Peace Prize

1967 is appointed research professor at the University of California, San Diego

1969 is appointed Professor of Chemistry at Stanford University

1970 publishes *Vitamin C and the Common Cold*

1979 publishes, with Ewan Cameron, *Vitamin C and Cancer*

1986 publishes *How to Live Longer and Feel Better*

1991 is diagnosed with cancer

1994 dies August 19 at Big Sur, California

Chemistry Timeline

440 B.C. Democritus proposes the concept of the atom as the smallest particle composing all things

250 B.C. Archimedes evaluates the relative density of bodies by observing their buoyancy in water

1144 A.D. Earliest dated alchemical treatise, *De compositione alchemiae* by Robert of Chester

1635 John Winthrop opens the first American chemical plant in Boston

1660 Robert Boyle finds that the volume of any gas at a constant temperature is inversely proportionate to the pressure

1766 Henry Cavendish discovers "inflammable air" (oxygen)

1771 Joseph Priestley demonstrates that oxygen is produced by plants and consumed by animals

1772 Daniel Rutherford describes "residual air" (first description of nitrogen)

1780 Lavoisier and Laplace conclude respiration is a form of combustion

1787 Jacque Charles studies volume changes of gases with changes in temperature

1789 Nicholas Le Blanc develops process to convert salt into soda ash

1810 Joseph Gay-Lussac deduces equations of alcoholic fermentation

1811 Amadeo Avagadro demonstrates that equal volumes of all gases under the same temperature and pressure contain the same number of molecules

1828 Friederich Wohler synthesizes the first organic compound from inorganic compounds

1835 Jons Berzelius publishes the first general theory of chemical catalysis

1845 Alfred Kolbe synthesizes acetic acid

1876 The American Chemical Society (ACS) is formed

1878 Josiah Gibbs develops the theory of chemical thermodynamics

1884 Arrhenius and Ostwald independently define acids as substances that release hydrogen ions when dissolved in water

1887 Emil Fischer elaborated the structural patterns of proteins

1895 Linde develops a process for liquefying air

1902 Arthur Noyes, MIT professor, establishes Research Laboratory of Physical Chemistry

1942 Enrico Fermi operates first man-made nuclear reactor

1953 Crick and Watson solve double helix structure of DNA

1959 Computer control of chemical processes gains credibility

1981 Chemical process simulation software is released for PCs; Binnig and Rohrer develop Scanning Tunnel Microscope that can resolve individual atoms on a surface

2001 Analyses of the human genome sequence published in February

2003 Expected completion date of the human genome project

Further Reading

For Young Readers:

Newton, David E. *Linus Pauling: Scientist and Advocate.* New York: Facts on File, 1994.

Patten, J.M. *Elements, Compounds and Mixtures.* Vero Beach, Florida: The Rourke Book Co., 1995.

Sherrow, Victoria. *Linus Pauling: Investigating the Magic Within.* Austin: Raintree/Steck-Vaughn, 1997.

White, Florence. *Linus Pauling: Scientist and Crusader.* New York: Walker and Co., 1980.

Works Consulted:

Hager, Tom. *Linus Pauling and the Chemistry of Life.* New York: Oxford University Press, 1998.

Mead, Clifford, ed. *Linus Pauling: Scientist and Peacemaker.* Corvallis: Oregon State University Press, 2001.

_____, ed. *The Pauling Catalogue: Ava Helen & Linus Pauling Papers at Oregon State University.* Kerr Special Library Collections, 1991.

Pauling, Linus. *Linus Pauling: In His Own Words: Selected Writings, Speeches, and Interviews.* New York: Touchstone Books, 1995.

Serafini, Anthony. *Linus Pauling: A Man and His Science.* New York: Paragon House, 1989.

On the Internet:

Linus Pauling, a Biography

http://www.woodrow.org/teachers/ci/1992/Pauling.html

Linus Pauling Interview: Conversations with History

http://globetrotter.berkeley.edu/conversations/Pauling/pauling1.html

Linus Pauling, profile and photos

http://www.archives.caltech.edu

Linus Pauling Interview with John L. Greenberg

http://resolver.caltech.edu/CaltechOH:OH_Pauling_L

Linus Pauling Institute - Biography

http://lpi.oregonstate.edu/lpbio2.html

HISTORICAL FOOTNOTE: The Paulings had four children. Linus Pauling, Jr., M.D., a psychiatrist, lives in Honolulu. Peter Pauling, Ph.D., a crystallographer and retired lecturer in chemistry, resides in Wales. Linda Pauling Kamb lives with her husband, a Caltech professor of geology, in the home originally built by her parents in the foothills above Pasadena. Crellin Pauling, Ph.D., was a professor of biology at San Francisco State University until his death in 1997. There are 15 grandchildren and 19 great-grandchildren.

The assets of the Linus Pauling Institute of Science and Medicine were used to establish the Linus Pauling Institute as a research institute at OSU in 1996 to investigate the function and role of micronutrients, phytochemicals and microconstituents of food in maintaining human health and preventing and treating disease; and to advance the knowledge in areas which were of interest to Linus Pauling through research and education. LPI continues to function as a working tribute to a great scientist, Linus Pauling.

Glossary

antioxidant – vitamin that helps prevent cell damage

atom – the smallest unit of an element that can exist either alone or in combination

bond – the force that holds two or more elements together to form a compound

chemistry – the science that studies the composition of substances

compound – two or more elements bonded to make a new substance

DNA – deoxyribonucleic acid; the substance from which genes are made

electron – the negatively charged ion that orbits the nucleus of an atom

element – any of more than 100 basic substances in which all atoms are alike and different from the atoms of all other elements

euphorius – the feeling of being happy or elated

fallout – the descent of particles to the earth after an explosion

gene – a part of DNA that contains chemical information needed to make a particular protein that controls our inherited characteristics

helix – a spiral shape

ion – an atom or group of atoms that carries a positive or negative electric charge as a result of having lost or gained one or more electrons

mixture – a combination of parts that can be easily separated

molecule – the smallest unit of a substance that has all the characteristics of that substance

nucleus – the central part of an atom containing most of its mass and having a positive charge

periodic table – the chart of all the elements according to their atomic weights

physics – the science that studies matter and motion

protein – the substance from which plants and animals are formed

quantum mechanics – the study of the behavior of subatomic particles

radioactivity – the process by which certain elements emit particles and/or rays when the nuclei of their atoms disintegrates

tetrahedron – a structure with four plane faces

X-ray crystallography – the process of directing an X-ray beam at a crystal so that the ray refracts into a distinctive pattern that reveals the structure of the crystal's molecules

Index